		DATE DUE	

ANCIENT CHINA

BY MARCIE FLINCHUM ATKINS

Essential Library

An Imprint of Abdo Publishing | www.abdopublishing.com

ANCIENT CHINA

BY MARCIE FLINCHUM ATKINS

CONTENT CONSULTANT

Jue Guo
Assistant Professor of Ancient China
Barnard College, Columbia University

www.abdopublishing.com

Published by Abdo Publishing, a division of ABDO, PO Box 398166, Minneapolis, Minnesota 55439. Copyright © 2015 by Abdo Consulting Group, Inc. International copyrights reserved in all countries. No part of this book may be reproduced in any form without written permission from the publisher. Essential Library™ is a trademark and logo of Abdo Publishing.

Printed in the United States of America, North Mankato, Minnesota

102014
012015

THIS BOOK CONTAINS
RECYCLED MATERIALS

Cover Photos: Yuri Yavnik/Shutterstock Images, background; Harley Couper/Shutterstock Images, foreground

Interior Photos: Yuri Yavnik/Shutterstock Images, 3; iStockphoto, 6–7, 11, 16–17, 43, 67, 86–87, 91, 92–93; World History Archive/Alamy, 8; Red Line Editorial, 12, 24; Lowell Georgia/Corbis, 21; Sang Tan/AP Images, 26; National Palace Museum in Taipei, 27; Olaf Schubert/ImageBroker RM/ Glow Images, 28–29; Dave Bartruff/Corbis, 31; Chinese School/Musee Guimet, Paris, France/ Archives Charmet/Bridgeman Images, 33; B Christopher/Alamy, 35; Imaginechina/Corbis, 37, 97; Dorling Kindersley/Thinkstock, 38–39; Hemera/Thinkstock, 41; View Stock/Alamy, 45; Huang Tao/ Imaginechina/AP Images, 49; Yang Xun/Imaginechina/AP Images, 50–51; Keren Su/Corbis, 53, 83; Asian Art & Archaeology, Inc./Corbis, 55; World History Archive/Newscom, 56–57; Ju Huanzong/ Xinhua Press/Corbis, 59; Shutterstock Images, 62–63; akg-images/Laurent Lecat/Newscom, 65; akg-images/Mark De Fraeye/Newscom, 73; Viktor Korotayev/Reuters/Corbis, 74–75; Yi Lu/Viewstock/ Corbis, 78; Yan Sheng/CNImaging/Newscom, 81

Editor: Lauren Coss
Series Designer: Jake Nordby

Library of Congress Control Number: 2014943837

Cataloging-in-Publication Data

Atkins, Marcie Flinchum.
 Ancient China / Marcie Flinchum Atkins.
   p. cm. -- (Ancient civilizations)
ISBN 978-1-62403-536-4 (lib. bdg.)
Includes bibliographical references and index.
1. China--Civilization--To 221 B.C.--Juvenile literature. 2. China--Civilization-- 221 B.C.-960 A.D.-- Juvenile literature. 3. China--History--Juvenile literature. 4. China--Social life and customs--Juvenile literature. I. Title.
931--dc23

                                                                2014943837

CONTENTS

CHAPTER 1

CHINA'S FIRST EMPEROR

In 246 BCE, the state of Qin (pronounced "chin") in northwestern China declared a new ruler. The new king, Ying Zheng, was only 13 years old, but he would rule over the small, powerful territory held by the Qin people.

Emperor Qin Shihuangdi, as Ying Zheng became known, was responsible for building a portion of China's famous Great Wall.

Zheng may have been young, but he was ambitious. At the time, China was divided into seven separate states—Qin, Han, Zhao, Chu, Yan, Wei, and Qi—each controlled by a different ruler. Zheng wanted to rule over all the Chinese states. The Qin army was better supplied, better organized, and faster than the armies from the other states. With the help of his adviser, Li Si, Zheng used his military might to conquer the states one by one. By 221 BCE, ancient China was under Zheng's control.

Zheng changed his name to Qin Shihuangdi. *Di* was a name used for the gods. The title *Huangdi* meant he thought of himself as a living god. His new name Shihuangdi meant "first sovereign emperor," and he became the first Chinese ruler with the title of emperor.[1]

GOVERNING CHINA

Qin Shihuangdi's realm spanned most of the eastern part of modern China, and governing the region was an enormous task. Qin Shihuangdi believed he was the supreme ruler, and if his subjects disagreed with him, they were punished. This strict manner of governing was known as legalism. Qin Shihuangdi ordered that many things become standardized including weights, measurements, and writing. He also improved the roadways so citizens could easily move from place to place, which improved trading. He ordered a canal built to connect several of China's major rivers. Qin Shihuangdi also built a wall, which would eventually become part of the Great Wall, to protect his kingdom from attacks from the Huns, a group of nomads from the north.

Although Qin Shihuangdi made great strides in unifying ancient China and advancing the region's infrastructure, he was a strict ruler. As part of Qin Shihuangdi's legalist thinking, he viewed scholars as a threat because they might oppose his rule. Historians believe Qin Shihuangdi buried more than 400 scholars alive because they opposed his way of thinking.

A CLOSER LOOK

TERRA-COTTA WARRIORS

In 1974, farmers were digging a well near Xi'an, China. While digging, they unearthed a strange statue. The men reported the findings, and the Chinese government organized an archaeological team to unearth the statue. Much to their surprise, archaeologists found more than 6,000 life-sized terra-cotta soldiers and thousands of weapons.[2] Inscriptions on some of the bronze weapons revealed the archaeologists had discovered Qin Shihuangdi's tomb.

Qin Shihuangdi forced workers to build a tomb to defend him in the afterlife. In addition to terra-cotta warriors meant to protect the emperor, the pits housed clay chariots, horses, and cavalrymen. Great care was taken to create the burial ground. Of the thousands of life-sized statues, no two are alike. To create such a vast and intricate clay army, many laborers were worked literally to death. Those who remained alive at Qin Shihuangdi's death were buried with him.

Archaeologists have found evidence of great technological and military advancements in the pits. They learned about ancient Chinese

techniques for creating weapons and how advanced they were compared with their European counterparts. Today China's ghost army is a tourist attraction and one of the greatest archaeological finds ever.

In 213 BCE, Qin Shihuangdi ordered many of the country's books burned. Qin Shihuangdi gave the scholars one month to bring him all of the books. Scholars owned these books because they had been handed down to them from previous generations. At this time, books were not made of paper. Instead, words were written on silk or on bamboo strips tied together. Any books on history and literature were destroyed. Qin Shihuangdi spared books about technology, divination, agriculture, and medicine because they might be needed for practical uses. He also kept one copy of each of the destroyed books in the imperial library, but the copies were destroyed when the library burned down in 206 BCE.

ANCIENT CHINA DURING THE QIN DYNASTY, CIRCA 210 BCE

QIN

N

Qin Shihuangdi may have been a stern ruler, but he unified ancient China in a way no leader had been able to before. He was also China's namesake. The name *China* comes from *Qin*. Qin Shihuangdi's system of bureaucracy also served as a model for future rulers. He died in 210 BCE, and the Qin dynasty collapsed only four years later. In 206 BCE, the Han dynasty came to power, ruling the ancient civilization Qin Shihuangdi had unified.

HOW ANCIENT IS ANCIENT CHINA?

Ancient China's history goes back thousands of years, well before Qin Shihuangdi came into power. This makes it one of the most ancient civilizations in the world. However, unlike many other ancient civilizations that exist only in artifacts and memory today, the civilization that formed in ancient China has existed uninterrupted for thousands of years. The rich culture that developed in China so long ago has evolved into modern Chinese culture.

Who Are the Chinese?

Chinese culture is a blend of many groups from history. Today, the Chinese government recognizes 56 ethnic groups, but 92 percent of the Chinese people today are part of the Han ethnic group, which is the largest ethnic group in the world.[3] The Han people are named after the Han dynasty, which ruled from 206 BCE to 220 CE, following the Qin dynasty's fall. Historians believe the Han people originally lived near the Huang River.

Chinese Dynasties

Chinese history is tracked by its dynasties rather than by particular periods. A dynasty is a society that was ruled for a particular period by a family or clan. The leadership of the Chinese dynasties was passed down from father to son, or older brother to younger brother. When the quality of government declined, peasants rebelled. Soon, the old dynasty would be overthrown and a new dynasty took its place. Many Chinese dynasties lasted several hundred years.

Many of the cultures known as ancient China were sandwiched between or around two major rivers, the Huang (or Yellow) River and the Yangtze River. People settled near the rivers because the land was fertile and good for farming.

By the 2000s BCE, these villages had organized into many small states. A series of dynasties may have begun as early as 2205 BCE. Many historians believe the Xia dynasty was the first of these dynasties. The dynasty is recorded in many historic sources, but archaeologists have not been able to find concrete proof of its existence. Following the Xia dynasty, different dynasties ruled parts of China for thousands of years until it was unified by the Qin dynasty. After the fall of the Qin dynasty, ancient China passed from emperor to emperor and dynasty to dynasty. Unlike many European leaders, ancient China's emperors focused on bringing the many cultures and regions of ancient China together instead of expanding China's geography outward. In 1276 CE, Mongol invaders successfully overthrew the Song dynasty, ending more than 1,400 years of consecutive Chinese rule.

Beginning during the Song dynasty, and lasting from approximately 1000 CE to 1500 CE, China was a world leader in economic and technological development. Many historians see modern China as beginning during this time.

"The Chinese had a very cultured and civilized society. Song Dynasty silks, for example, were remarkably advanced. The Chinese were using very sophisticated looms with up to 1,800 moving parts. China was simply far more developed technologically and culturally than any state in the West."[4]

—Robin Yates, China expert

CHAPTER 2

A LONG HISTORY

hinese history goes back thousands of years. Humans most likely came to the area between 30,000 and 50,000 years ago. In approximately 10,000 BCE, peoples who had previously been nomadic began settling down, building villages, and creating tools. In several thousand years, these villages became

The Yangtze River was an important waterway in ancient China from the civilization's earliest days.

Neolithic China

China's Neolithic period, during the latter part of the Stone Age, lasted from approximately 10,000 BCE to 2000 BCE. During this time, nomadic hunters and gatherers settled into a more permanent village-type life. They began farming millet in the north and rice in the south. Archaeologists have even found jade and metalworking evidence dating back to this time. Tombs from the era contain large amounts of highly developed pottery. The clay pottery used in burial rituals often features red and black line paintings.

vast kingdoms ruled by powerful dynasties. Each dynasty is associated with particular advancements or accomplishments.

THE FIRST DYNASTIES

The dynasties of ancient China covered a portion of what we now know as modern China. Each state occupied certain territories until the unification of China under the Qin dynasty.

The mythical Xia dynasty was likely one of the earliest dynasties, lasting from approximately 2100 BCE to 1600 BCE. Historians believe the mostly agricultural Xia society may have settled near the Huang River, where archaeologists have uncovered artifacts including bronzes, copper, jade, and pottery. Little concrete information is known about this mysterious dynasty, or whether it truly existed.

Historians do know that between 1800 BCE and 1600 BCE, the Shang dynasty came into power in the northeast part of China, with the Huang and Yangtze Rivers running through the middle. This powerful dynasty lasted hundreds of years, until approximately the 1040s BCE. The Shang dynasty was an agricultural society with farmers growing crops and raising animals. People also relied on hunting for food. They worshiped their deceased ancestors and sought their advice.

Archaeologists have discovered oracle bones from this period. Oracles used these bones to seek answers about the future. The oracle carved the questions into the bones and then performed a ceremony to obtain answers. The oracle bones show the Shang people had a developed writing system.

Folklore or History?: The Xia Dynasty

The Xia dynasty is thought to be the first Chinese dynasty, but to date, archaeologists cannot verify its existence. However, some archaeological finds may give credibility to the reality of the Xia dynasty. Archaeologists discovered bamboo strips, which people used as books at that time, inscribed with stories about the Xia. But these stories were written down more than 2,000 years after the dynasty ended. The Xia history was first passed down by word of mouth. Historians in the 1920s doubted the stories because the written records did not match the artifacts. However, in the 1950s, archaeologists found what was possibly one of the Xia's dynasty's nine capitals in the Henan Province. Carbon dating places the city between the Neolithic and Shang dynasty periods. Western scholars believe more evidence is needed to determine whether the Xia dynasty really existed because no written records match the archaeological findings. Some Chinese scholars insist that the Xia dynasty did, in fact, exist.

A CLOSER LOOK

TALKING BONES

For many years, no one knew if the Shang dynasty was real or legendary. Then in the 1920s, archaeologists found more than 25,000 bones and turtle shells with writing and cracks on them near Anyang, the Shang capital.[1] The bones were from the shoulder blades of oxen.

Oracles used the bones to help the royal family contact their ancestors to ask them questions. The oracle carved the questions into the bones. Then, the oracle would take a hot poker and touch the shells or the bones until they cracked. The oracle interpreted the cracks to give an answer.

Based on the writings, historians know many of the questions concerned current and future events, such as who would win the war or whether the king would remain healthy. The questions also revealed a lot about farming methods, medicine, the legal system, and even textile production.

To date, more than 150,000 bones with writing have been found.[2] The bones are the earliest written records of Chinese history still in existence.

The Mandate of Heaven

When the Zhou dynasty overthrew the Shang dynasty, the Zhou used the "Mandate of Heaven" to justify their actions. The mandate said a ruler kept his power only until heaven became upset with him. Natural disasters, military defeat, or the inability to produce an heir were all signs an emperor was not fit to rule. Because there was only one heaven, only one emperor could rule at a time. If he failed to look after the people, he would lose his right to rule. If an emperor was overthrown, it was a sign that heaven was upset with him. The doctrine, which began in the 700s BCE, was accepted throughout much of ancient Chinese history.

Bronze vessels from the time also include inscriptions. Both the oracle bones and bronze vessels give clues about what was important to the Shang people based on the types of questions they asked.

The Zhou dynasty came into power in 1046 BCE after overthrowing the Shang dynasty. The Zhou dynasty lasted for hundreds of years in the northeastern part of China, until 256 BCE. This dynasty created the foundation for the politics and culture of China for the next 2,000 years. During the Zhou dynasty, much progress was made in agriculture. The Zhou built canals, damming the rivers to help irrigate the crops more consistently. The irrigation system meant reliable crops, and the Zhou population increased with more food available.

A TIME OF CONFLICT

During the Zhou dynasty, the various states of China struggled for power. The era from 770 BCE to 476 BCE is known as the Spring and Autumn period. This was a time of intense power struggle between many small states. The great philosopher Confucius lived from 551 BCE to 479 BCE. His way of thinking inspired Confucianism, one of the main philosophical and ethical systems of thought in Chinese history. It emphasized moral perfection and promoted the good of the people over the good of the individual. During the Spring and Autumn period, the Chinese began using coins as money. Before this time, shells and silk had been used as money.

The year 475 BCE marks the beginning of the Warring States period. By this time, the many small states had been organized into seven larger states, which fought for supreme rule of ancient China. It was a time of disunity because of war, but it was also a time of cultural advancement. The constant state of war forced competition between the states. Each state tried to build the strongest army and improve its technology and economy. At this time, weapons and tools for farming were mostly fashioned from iron, a technology that continued to improve from the Zhou dynasty onward. The Warring States period ended with the unification of ancient China under the Qin dynasty in 221 BCE.

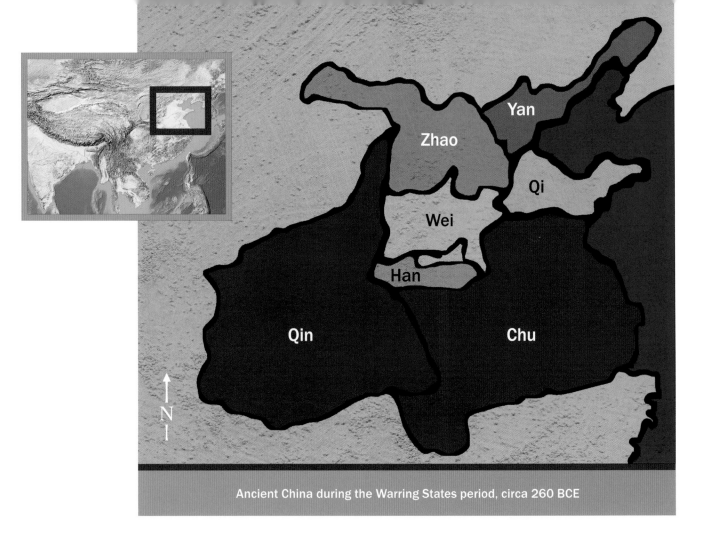

Ancient China during the Warring States period, circa 260 BCE

A UNIFIED CHINA

Under the rule of Qin Shihuangdi, the Qin dynasty unified the country, taking over many smaller states and creating a government with supreme rule. However, the Qin dynasty lasted only 14 years. After Qin Shihuangdi's death, his advisers fought, and soon the Han dynasty came into power.

The Han dynasty ruled nearly uninterrupted for more than 400 years. Chinese culture flourished during this time. Confucianism became more accepted, and Buddhism, a religion that had originated in India, also began flourishing. The Silk Road, a major trading route for many goods, developed, connecting China to the Mediterranean Sea. This allowed Chinese ideas, discoveries, and inventions to reach other parts of the world.

Paper and porcelain also developed during this dynasty. The Chinese invented new methods for preserving foods, including pickling and salting techniques. They also established civil service exams for court officials, which meant one could obtain a position in the government through hard work and skill, rather than only by birthright, as had been the case in the past.

THE SIX DYNASTIES PERIOD AND BEYOND

From 220 to 589 CE, different dynasties ruled ancient China, but none ruled for very long. Invaders from the northern border took over northern China, and a succession of dynasties ruled over southern China. But Chinese culture and art blossomed despite the political divisions. Celadon, a type of glazed pottery, was invented. More sophisticated sculptures, paintings, and calligraphy appeared during this time. Buddhism also thrived. Gradually,

China reunified under the short-lived Sui dynasty, which began ruling northern China in 581.

Ancient Chinese art continued to thrive during the Tang dynasty, which lasted from 618 to 907. Poetry and literature flourished during this time. The Tang dynasty also made advances in pottery, and potters created multicolored glazes. Printed books were invented during the Tang dynasty. Wu Zhao, the first female emperor, reigned from 690 to 705.

During the years between the Tang dynasty and the beginning of the Song dynasty, in 960, a period known as the Five Dynasties and Ten Kingdoms represented a quick succession of rulers. The country split into at least ten kingdoms. When the Song dynasty took control, it ruled a region covering most of eastern and central

Buddhism was common during the Tang dynasty, and many artifacts were created depicting the Buddha.

Mongolian leader Genghis Khan led the Mongol invasion of China.

China for more than 300 years. This was a time of advancement for the Chinese. The economy grew with trading and the expansion of the country. Neo-Confucianism, a hybrid of Confucian, Buddhist, and Taoist ideas, became part of the civil service examinations.

However, a foreign power would soon seize China. Mongol warriors invaded China from the north in 1211, gradually taking over more and more of the region. By 1279, Mongol invaders had successfully taken over all of China.

CHAPTER 3

IMPERIAL GOVERNMENT

Much of what we know about ancient Chinese government dates to the imperial era. In imperial China, an emperor ruled the whole land. China's imperial era began when Qin emperor Qin Shihuangdi gave himself the title of emperor. Emperors continued ruling China until 1911.

A modern statue of Qin Shihuangdi stands near his tomb in Xi'an.

Ancient China's imperial government was based on legalism. Legalism meant the government was firmly in control and the government's prosperity trumped the individual welfare of the common people. Those who tried to defy the government faced severe punishment.

THE IMPERIAL COURT

The emperor was the head of ancient China, but he appointed many people to his court to help him rule. The court members worked directly for the emperor and served his advisers in religious, military, and economic matters. Members of the royal family, eunuchs, bureaucrats, and scholars were all part of an emperor's court.

Eunuchs were male court officials who had been mutilated so they could no longer produce children. Because eunuchs could not have heirs, the emperors believed there was no chance a eunuch would try to overthrow the government. However, many eunuchs wielded power in the court. Other eunuchs did jobs that ranged from cleaning the kitchens to serving as guards.

Scholars and bureaucrats also played an important role in imperial courts, particularly after the Qin dynasty. They were given places of authority and honor. If a son in an ancient Chinese family showed promise for learning and scholarship, that family would sacrifice everything so he

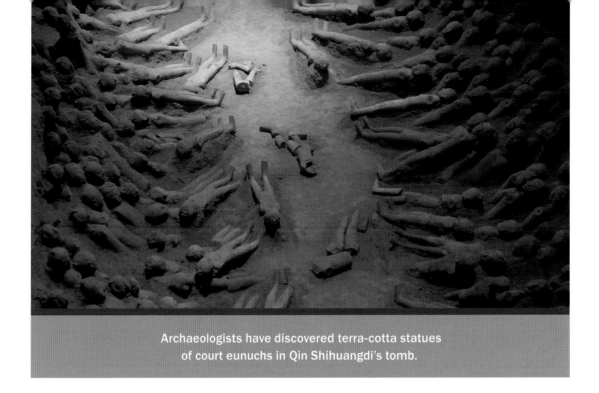

Archaeologists have discovered terra-cotta statues of court eunuchs in Qin Shihuangdi's tomb.

could study, write essays and poetry, and hopefully become a court scholar or bureaucrat.

The Han dynasty implemented a civil service exam. Those who wanted to serve in government positions would be appointed based on their knowledge of literature. Emperors wanted to draw the best talent into the government. Then the emperor's advisers could provide guidance based on their intellect alone, not based on their family loyalties.

THE POWER OF WOMEN

Men dominated much of ancient Chinese government. Boys were highly valued in ancient Chinese societies. Poor families who could not afford to raise many children sometimes resorted to killing baby girls. However, even in this male-dominated society, some women found ways to gain power. An empress dowager, the mother of an emperor, could temporarily be in charge if the emperor was a child or unable to rule for some other reason. Empress Wu Zhao was one of those empress dowagers; however, she took her role

Empress Wu Zhao

Empress Wu Zhao ruled ancient China from 690 to 705 CE. She was the only woman in ancient Chinese history to be truly in charge. She started by working her way up through the ranks. She became a concubine to Emperor Taizong of the Tang dynasty at age 14. After the emperor's death, she became a concubine to his heir, the new emperor, Gaozong. The emperor's wife, Empress Wang, did not have any children. However, Wu Zhao had several sons with the emperor. Wu Zhao encouraged the idea that one of them should be Gaozong's heir. She managed to demote Empress Wang. When the emperor had a stroke, Wu Zhao gained more power in his court.

In line to be the next emperor, Empress Wu Zhao's son was pushed out of the way by his own mother, and Empress Wu Zhao came to power in 690 CE. She accomplished many things in her rule, including military success, decreased taxation, and religious changes. She placed Buddhism over Taoism as the official religion. Scholarship and the arts flourished during her reign.

a step further by declaring herself fully in charge, eventually becoming emperor.

Some women gained power by marrying or becoming the concubines of successful men. Many Chinese emperors had thousands of concubines. Rulers found security in fathering children with concubines, ensuring their reign would continue after their death through one of their many heirs. Concubines also found they could gain power in their roles. Because they were so close to the emperor, they sometimes influenced his decisions.

武瞾 士彟之女 壽八十二歲 古今無比

An artist's rendition of Empress Wu Zhao

TRADE AND THE SILK ROAD

Trading contributed to the economic success of ancient China during the Imperial era. Qin Shihuangdi's standardized measurement system helped make trade between different regions of China easier. Foods, such as fish, cattle, and salt, in addition to goods, including silk and iron, crisscrossed the empire.

The Chinese also traded with other civilizations using the Silk Road, which was established during the Han dynasty. The Silk Road was a set of multiple trade routes spanning 4,000 miles (6,400 km).[1] Caravans loaded with

Silk Culture

Silk production began in ancient China in the 2000s BCE. It became an important part of Chinese culture. The Chinese kept the silk-making process a secret for more than 2,000 years. Creating silk cloth was more than weaving silk threads. Silk making was extremely complex, and women did nearly all of the work. Silk comes from a fiber produced by silkworms, which eat the leaves of mulberry trees. The temperature and humidity must be kept even for the silkworm to survive. Eventually, the silkworms spin cocoons made of silk threads. To get the threads off, the ancient silk makers boiled the silkworms and then unrolled the silk strands from the cocoons.

It took nearly 2,000 silkworms to make one pound (0.45 kg) of silk.[2] After unrolling the cocoons, silk makers twisted the silk strands together and dyed them different colors. Then they wove the strands to make cloth.

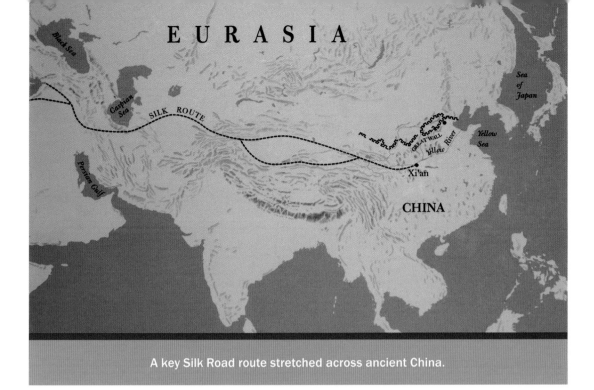

A key Silk Road route stretched across ancient China.

goods could travel along the road from Japan and China, across central Asia, south into India, and west across the Middle East to the Mediterranean Sea and the Roman Empire, where Chinese luxury items were in demand. Silk was only one of the items traded along the Silk Road routes. The Chinese also traded jade, gems, glass, lacquer ware, spices, incense, tea, ivory, cotton, wool, linen, musical instruments, paper, silver, and gold. In exchange, the Chinese received goods including wool, linen, amber, wine, and gold coins from the Romans. The Silk Road improved the Chinese economy, and it brought ideas, religions, and foreigners into China.

CURRENCY

Silk was more than just a good to be traded. Chinese people wrote on silk before the invention of paper. They also sometimes used silk as currency from the Zhou dynasty through the Tang dynasty. In addition to silk, shells served as ancient Chinese currency.

Coins were introduced just before the Warring States period. The first coins were made of bronze; later, coins came in iron. This type of currency was used until the early 1900s CE.

Paper banknotes first appeared in the 800s CE. Early paper banknotes, called "flying money," were written for different amounts.[3] People with cash

The Grand Canal

China had two big rivers, the Huang and the Yangtze, which served as major waterways for transportation. Connecting these rivers to each other allowed the Chinese to link different parts of the empire. In the north, farmers grew wheat, and in the south, they grew rice. Canals provided a way to exchange goods between the two regions. The canals also increased the military power of the government because the military could more easily transport troops and supplies along the waterways.

Workers dug the first canals during the Qin dynasty. Sui dynasty workers completed the Grand Canal project between 605 and 609 CE, linking the Huang and Yangtze Rivers. In all, the canal ran more than 1,200 miles (1,900 km).[4]

Ancient Chinese coins had square holes in the middle so the owner could string them on a rope.

could deposit the currency in the capital cities in exchange for a paper certificate. They could take this certificate back to the capital and be able to pay for things they needed.

CHAPTER 4

LIFE IN ANCIENT CHINA

Daily life in ancient China varied greatly depending on whether a person was a noble or a farmer or a man or a woman. Rich or poor, family relationships were highly valued in ancient Chinese culture. The family unit did not consist only of a husband, wife, and children. Instead, several generations often lived together. Marriages were arranged early in a child's

Citizens of ancient Chinese cities performed a wide variety of roles and jobs.

Growing Rice

Rice has been grown in China since Neolithic times. It may have been cultivated as early as the 6000s BCE. Rice grows most easily in standing water. The farmers used a foot-powered pump to bring water from a canal or river to flood the rice field. Rice seedlings were planted by hand, and growing rice was very labor intensive. The Song discovered a different variety of rice, native to Southeast Asia, worked better for the environment of South China.

life and were designed to continue the family line. Elders expected respect, and it was a common practice to pray to and worship one's ancestors. As they do today, the ancient Chinese put their surname first, before their personal name, which showed the great importance of the family.

AGRICULTURE

The literature and paintings of ancient China depicted the lives of rulers and aristocrats. Historians do not have as much information about what daily life was like for commoners, except for the few artifacts uncovered in archaeological digs. Historians know farming played an important role in ancient Chinese society because of tools and pottery found in large village sites near the Huang River.

Agriculture was important across different regions of China. More than one-half of the crops we eat today originally came from Asia. Those thought to originate in China include millet, chestnut, walnuts, soybeans, Chinese cabbage, some citrus fruits, and many more. Millet, a type of grain,

was one of the main crops in ancient China. Rice grew naturally along the Huang River and was likely harvested as early as 8000 BCE. Starting in the 200s BCE, the Chinese irrigated their crops using canals.

In rural areas, daily life centered on farming tasks. Men and women typically each had their own jobs. Men worked the soil with hoes and wooden spades. They tilled the fields, hunted, and fished. Women spent their

The Importance of Tea

Tea came to China, probably from Burma, no later than the early first century CE. It was cultivated and prized in China. The ancient Chinese thought tea detoxified the body and gave the drinker energy. During the Tang dynasty, people consumed tea as a social activity or to relax. Poets drank tea while composing their poetry. Author Lu Yu wrote the first book about tea, translated as *Classic of Tea*, during the Tang dynasty. It detailed tea's unique properties and how to properly make tea. Tea was sometimes stored in bamboo tubes, and later, during the Song dynasty, it was pressed into bricks for transport.

time cooking, making wine, raising silkworms for silk production, and weaving. In agricultural Chinese society, an oxcart was the most common mode of transportation. An ox pulled a covered two-wheeled cart and helped farmers move agricultural products from rural areas to cities where they could be sold.

CITY LIFE

Many ancient Chinese lived in bustling cities. Cities were centers of government and trade. They were home to government officials, scholars, merchants, and craftsmen.

Each dynasty established its own capital for the government. Many dynastic rulers chose Chang'an, now known as Xi'an, a city located in the middle of China. The Western Han, Sui, and Tang dynasties all used Chang'an for their capital. During the Tang dynasty, walls built to keep invaders out surrounded Chang'an. Approximately 1 million people lived in Chang'an, likely making it the largest city in the world at the time.[1]

Walls still surround Xi'an, once an important capital in ancient China.

Walls wrapped around most ancient Chinese cities and villages. In fact, in Chinese, the word for *city* literally means "walls and markets." Most cities also housed marketplaces. Items for sale were grouped together, so there were rows selling meat, fish, vegetables, medicines, ready-made clothing, silk, gold, silver, axes, and bridles and saddles.

CLOTHING

The type of clothing a person wore indicated his or her status. Both men and women wore tunics, loose clothing that resembled a long shirt and usually reached the knees. The style depended on the person's place in society. Some wore tunics with pants, whereas others wore floor-length robes. The wealthier a person was, the fancier his or her clothing. Most common people wore clothing made of cotton or hemp. Only the wealthy could afford silk clothing. The ancient Chinese dyed clothing with four colors—red, blue, yellow, and green.

PASTIMES

Fun was also an important part of daily life in ancient China, particularly for the wealthy. The ancient Chinese were the inventors of many games and

Foot Binding

During the Song dynasty, it became common for young girls, starting from the age of four or six, to wrap their feet in strips of cloth. This made their toes curl up and their feet appear smaller. The girls' own mothers often broke their feet, over and over again, wrapping after each time. The breaking made the foot smaller and smaller, bringing the toes closer to the heels and preventing further growth. Girls believed the painful foot-binding practice made their feet look dainty, beautiful, and more appealing to men. Girls continued wrapping their feet until approximately age 16, but by then, their feet were permanently deformed, making walking difficult. The custom may have started in the late Tang dynasty with a concubine wrapping her feet like a dancer. One legend says that it started as early as the Shang dynasty by an empress who had a deformed foot. The practice was banned in 1912.

activities still popular today. Common pastimes included soccer, card games, and playing with yo-yos.

Ancient China is credited with inventing the game of soccer. The sport originated in the Shandong Province of eastern China in the 200s or 100s BCE. The ancient Chinese called the game *cuju*. It was played for fun and during military exercises.

Playing cards originated in China in the 800s CE. They were made from thick paper two inches (5 cm) high by one inch (2.5 cm) wide.[2] Craftsmen printed the cards using

A modern painting shows ancient Chinese men playing soccer during the Song dynasty.

wood-cut blocks and then colored them by hand, sometimes with characters from novels.

The Chinese invented the *Kongzhu*, or yo-yo, more than 1,000 years ago. The yo-yos were made of bamboo attached to a string. Skilled Kongzhu players could make the yo-yo do more than 1,000 tricks.

CHINESE CALENDAR

Although the ancient Chinese invented many modern pastimes, daily life for many people revolved around farming. Ancient Chinese culture depended on agriculture, and agriculture depended on the calendar. Planting and harvesting activities centered on the solar and lunar cycles recorded on ancient Chinese calendars. In the thousands of years of Chinese history, different dynasties from the Han to the Qin observed the solar and lunar positions and calculated the revolution of the earth around the sun. The ancient Chinese calendar had 12 months in a year and 29 to 30 days in a month, with a total of 354 days. However, every two or three years, a month was added, giving the year 384 or 385 days. The calendar was often reset with each emperor, and regions used it differently. Now the Chinese government does not reset the calendar based on a new leader. They use the Gregorian calendar, the calendar used by the Western world, for most time tracking. However, the lunar and solar calendars continue to determine many traditional Chinese holidays.

CHINESE NEW YEAR

The Chinese New Year, also called the Spring Festival, was based on the lunar calendar. It began in the middle of the twelfth month and ended in the middle of the first full moon of the first month. This fell between January 21 and February 21. It was the most important holiday in ancient China and a time to honor gods and ancestors.

Before the celebrations began, the houses needed cleaning to rid them of *huiqi*, "unfavorable breaths," and to please the gods that inspected the houses. During the celebrations, people offered food and other sacrifices to the gods and ancestors. Scrolls were printed with lucky messages, and children received money from their elders. Firecrackers frightened away evil spirits. Food was, and still remains, an important part of the celebration. Eating long noodles in the beginning of the festival

Lantern Festival

The Lantern Festival was the first celebration of the year, celebrated during the first full moon after the Chinese New Year. This festival dates back to the Han dynasty. People jump over fire to get rid of bad luck and light lanterns after dark. Some of the traditional lanterns include riddles on them, and lanterns shaped like the segments of dragons are used in a dragon dance as part of the festivities. The festival is still celebrated in China today.

symbolizes long life. On New Year's Eve at midnight, families eat traditional round dumplings shaped like the full moon.

Another ancient Chinese festival, the Dragon Boat Festival, is still popular today. The festival has its roots in the 300s BCE. At the time, a minister named Qu Yuan had been banished by the emperor. Despite his exile, Qu Yuan wrote poems about his love for his country, but he eventually became so distraught he drowned himself. The common people so admired Qu Yuan they wanted his drowned body to be respected, not eaten by dragons or fish. So people decorated their boats like other dragons, racing them up and down the river. They beat gongs and drums to scare away the dragons.

BURIAL CUSTOMS

Ancient Chinese burials were also steeped in tradition. Much of what archaeologists know about ancient Chinese culture comes from studying ancient tombs. Chinese built their tombs underground, and some included multiple decorated rooms, particularly those of the Shang dynasty. The wealthy and powerful were buried with many valuable possessions because they believed they would continue in the same social status in the afterlife. Items such as weapons, bells, knives, sculptures, tools, and pottery are common objects modern archaeologists find in tombs. Wine was also placed in tombs so the deceased could hold honorary banquets for ancestors.

Sometimes servants were buried alive in the tombs of royalty as a sacrifice to honor the dead. Empty wine vessels and cups are also often found scattered in the graves. At the end of the funeral, mourners drank the wine and tossed the wine cup into the grave. The mourners paid respect to the dead by leaving objects to place in the grave.

An ancient Chinese tomb dating back at least 1,500 years was one of several discovered in the early 2000s.

CHAPTER 5

ARTISTIC TREASURES

A wide variety of art existed across ancient China. Ancient Chinese art included forms ranging from elaborate calligraphy to paintings to pottery. This art was both beautiful and practical. Many of these artifacts have been discovered in archaeological sites in China.

Many forms of ancient Chinese art, particularly pottery, have been excavated from tombs.

Lacquer

The lacquer tree is common in China at high altitudes of 3,000 to 7,500 feet (900 to 2,300 m). The tree contains a unique resin that was used as a varnish, or a plastic-like coating, as early as the Neolithic period. The resin is gray in color but darkens when it is exposed to air. After the resin was filtered and boiled it became a pale amber color. Vegetable or mineral pigments could change the color. Chinese artisans applied lacquer in thin layers to bamboo, bronze, clay, leather, paper, wooden tablets, silk, and pottery. Once dry, the lacquered objects became heat and water resistant. Some of the lacquer ware objects have survived for many centuries.

POTTERY

Pottery was one of the oldest forms of art in ancient China. Pottery has been found in archaeological sites dating back to Neolithic times. Artisans decorated terra-cotta pottery with designs or paintings of animals. Ancient Chinese craftsmen began using potter's wheels as early as the 2000s BCE, which made sculpting much faster. During the Tang dynasty potters began using multicolored glazes. The three colors available likely came from metal oxides used in the glazes—iron, which produced a yellow or brown color; copper, which produced a green or brown color; and cobalt, which produced the rare blue color. Lacquer ware became more widely used during the Han dynasty. The common terra-cotta pottery, which had been used since Neolithic times, declined in production, except for everyday items.

In the 200s CE, the Chinese developed porcelain, often called "china" for its country of origin. A very thin, delicate, purified clay was used to make porcelain. When the purified clay was fired at a higher temperature, it became translucent.

BRONZE AND JADE

The Bronze Age in China began in approximately 2000 BCE. During this time, the Chinese discovered ways to combine copper and tin to make bronze. The ores were heated over very high heat and poured into clay molds to make the shape desired. After cooling, artisans broke the molds apart.

Chinese craftsmen cast vessels for wine and food. Some of the vessels had legs on the bottom so a flame could be placed under the legs to warm the food. Other vessels for wine were in the shapes of animals. People during the Zhou dynasty used bronze to make boxes for food offerings for their

This bronze deer was uncovered in Qin Shihuangdi's tomb.

53

ancestors. They also made ceremonial tools and weapons. These bronze items were meant for ceremonial uses, not as everyday tools. One Shang king's wife had more than 200 bronze pieces in her tomb.[1]

Ancient Chinese artisans also worked with jade. This gemstone is usually a green color. It was probably cut out of large slabs of the mineral nephrite found in riverbeds beginning in the 3000s BCE, and it remained an important gemstone throughout ancient Chinese history. Jade carvings have been uncovered at many ancient Chinese archaeological sites. Jade disks, masks, and ceremonial items were carved with intricate designs. Owning bracelets, pendants, and head ornaments made out of jade indicated the wearer was of a high social status. Jade was also commonly included with burial items.

LIFE IN PAINTINGS

Traditional Chinese paintings often showcase the natural world. They feature landscapes, birds, flowers, or bamboo. The paintings were usually made on silk or paper. Artists used brushes, ink, and watercolor washes.

Such paintings reached their peak during the Song dynasty. Song artist Zhang Zeduan painted on horizontal scrolls. His work often depicted daily life in the city. It showed performers, streets, boats, restaurants, and life along the river.

THE JOY AND PLEASURE OF MUSIC

Music was an important part of life in ancient China. The Chinese character for *music* could also mean "joy," "pleasure," or "entertainment."

In 1978, 64 bells dating to the 400s BCE were found in an archaeological site near Hubei Province, in eastern China.[2] Each bell was marked with its musical note. But they had no clappers on the inside as Western bells had. Instead, the bells were struck on the outside with a mallet. In addition to the bells, stone chimes, bronze drums, string instruments, and bamboo flutes dating from the Zhou dynasty have been excavated.

People during the Han dynasty believed music had great moral power and affected people of all levels. They thought that for all to live in harmony, music should be a part of life.

Drums were important instruments in ancient Chinese music. This bronze, double-faced drum dates from the Shang dynasty.

A CLOSER LOOK

JADE *BI*

The ancient Chinese created artifacts known as *bi* out of jade. These flat discs with holes in their centers were believed to have a connection to immortality. They may also have been symbolic of the heavens or the sun. They were placed on the body during burial, looking like large necklace pendants.

The exact size, shape, and characteristics of a person's bi reflected his or her status and wealth. Some bi had knobs on them in decorative patterns. Others had illustrations. Jade bi have been found in burial sites near the Yangtze River dating to the Neolithic period, approximately 3300 BCE to 2250 BCE. They were later used by the Shang and Zhou dynasties. Much later, their use was revived during the Ming dynasty, which began in the 1300s CE, and the Qing dynasty, which began in the 1600s.

During the Han dynasty, government officials created an Office of Music to collect popular ballads and other songs and organize musical performances.

ANCIENT CHINESE HOUSES

Similar to other ancient Chinese art, Chinese architecture strived to be in harmony with nature. Houses were often built with wood, tile, plaster, mud, and stone. Thatched or tile roofing was also common on homes. Typically the buildings wrapped around a central courtyard. Some larger buildings were multistory and included watchtowers. Literature from ancient times describes grand palaces. Because most ancient Chinese buildings were built of wood and other materials that did not last, none still stand today. Historians learned about these houses through archaeological digs that uncovered parts of ancient buildings, such as walls, bases for columns, and ceramic tiles. Archaeologists also found models of buildings in tombs.

A few stone pagodas from the 500s and 600s CE still stand. The pagoda originated in India. The Chinese pagoda typically had a tall pointed spire on top. Usually constructed as an act of devotion or good luck, the pagoda could also be used as a watchtower. Pagodas were circular or octagonal.

CHINESE WRITING

One of China's most enduring art forms is its writing. The written language has been in use for at least 3,500 years, making it one of the oldest written

The work of Zhang Xu, a famous calligrapher from the Tang dynasty, can still be viewed at the Zhejiang Provincial Museum in Hangzhou, China.

languages in continuous use. It is written vertically and read from right to left. Chinese writing does not use an alphabet. Instead, it uses pictographs (picture symbols), ideographs (idea symbols), and phonemic graphs (sound symbols). Most words in Chinese are a combination of two to three characters, and each character is a combination of several standard strokes. The Chinese language has thousands of characters writers must memorize.

Writing itself was an art form in ancient China. Calligraphy was the art of writing using a brush and ink. The Chinese saw calligraphy as a way to achieve inner harmony and clear the mind. Calligraphers were great artists, but they were also respected as great thinkers of their time. In the Tang dynasty, one needed to be a skilled calligrapher to obtain a government post.

LITERATURE

The first Chinese books probably were made of bamboo or silk. Evidence of Chinese writing exists from the Shang dynasty. Fiction began in the 300s BCE and included fables and stories with dialogue. In the 200s BCE, the Qin dynasty standardized more than 3,000 characters in the Chinese language. This made it easier for people from across China to communicate with one another. However, Emperor Qin Shihuangdi burned thousands of books, destroying much of Chinese literature. After the book burning, thousands of books had to be reconstructed. The Han dynasty tried to restore the texts. These writings were likely reconstructed from oral histories or from books hidden during the burning.

Scholar Xu Shen compiled one of the first dictionaries in roughly 100 CE. Xu's dictionary included more than 9,000 characters, and it was one of the first dictionaries in the world.[3] He included the pronunciation of characters and the definitions of the words.

Poetry

The Chinese language lends itself to the lyrical qualities of rhyming, and poetry particularly flourished during the Tang dynasty. Poetry showed the character and integrity of the poet writing it. Most emperors supported poets, and many were even poets themselves. Three of the most well-known poets were Wang Wei (701–761 CE), Li Bai (701–762 CE), and Du Fu (712–770 CE). Wang's poetry usually took the form of a vignette about natural landscapes. Li wrote about the pleasures of life using imagery, painting pictures with his words. Du was known as the Sage of Poetry. He often wrote about landscapes and war.

CHAPTER 6

RELIGION, PHILOSOPHY, AND MYTHOLOGY

Spirituality and mythology have been deeply rooted in Chinese culture for thousands of years. In fact, many Western folktales, fairy tales, and myths known in modern times have ancient Chinese versions. For example, "The Tiger and the Grandmother" is a Chinese version of "Little Red Riding Hood." The oldest

The Chinese dragon, as shown on a modern wall in Beijing, China, has been an important part of Chinese mythology for thousands of years.

written version of "Cinderella" came from China. It was written by author Duan Chengshi and published in the 853 CE. The next earliest written version of "Cinderella" appeared in France in 1544.

China also has its own mythology, complete with mythological creatures. The dragon, unicorn, phoenix, and tortoise all play important roles in Chinese mythology. These creatures may look familiar to some of the creatures often associated with Western mythology, but the creatures of Chinese myth often have different characteristics.

The Chinese Zodiac

The ancient Chinese practiced astrology. In Chinese astrology, each year is named after an animal. The animals are the 12 signs that run along the path of the sun through the solar system. The legend of the years of each animal is rooted in Buddhism. One New Year, Buddha invited all of the animals to come to him, but only 12 animals showed up: the rat, ox, tiger, rabbit, dragon, snake, horse, sheep, monkey, rooster, dog, and pig. Each had a year named after it. The position of the sun, moon, and planets at the time of a person's birth determined his or her destiny.

As other zodiacs do, the Chinese zodiac explains the characteristics of the people born in that year. The ancient Chinese believed the year in which a person is born affected that person's fortune. Marriages and other major life decisions were made after consulting the zodiac.

A dragon adorns a bell dating from the Zhou dynasty.

DRAGON

The dragon has long been a symbol of Chinese culture. Dragon statues have been found dating back to Neolithic times. Dragons appeared on artwork and on buildings. Unlike Western dragons, ancient Chinese dragons were not seen as dangerous monsters. Instead, they were considered good luck.

The Han dynasty described the dragon as having the trunk of a snake, tail of a whale, face of a camel, claws of an eagle, feet of a tiger, scales of a carp, antlers of a deer, and ears of a bull. If you look closely at traditional Chinese dragon depictions, you may be able to see some of the features from other animals. Most dragons are shown with four claws because the five-clawed dragon was reserved for the emperor.

The ancient Chinese had many beliefs surrounding dragons. According to ancient Chinese legend, dragons ruled over the four seas around China: the East Sea, the West Sea, the South Sea, and the North Sea. Each sea had its own guardian dragon. The dragons lived in the water and could fly. Instead of fire, the dragons breathed clouds. They could become invisible or change shape and size. Sometimes they even appeared in human form.

Some people believed dragons caused floods when they traveled down a river. Farmers prayed to the dragons during a drought because legend said when dragons played in the clouds, they brought rain.

In ancient Chinese culture, dragons represented strength and goodness and were symbols of spring. Dragon processions, often held in the spring, ushered the return of the dragon that spent winter underground.

OTHER MYTHICAL CREATURES

The *fenghuang* is the most honored of all birds in Chinese mythology. It looks like a peacock, but it is immortal. It is the female counterpart to the dragon. The bird was the symbol of the empress and often appeared in ancient Chinese ceremonial costumes. According to ancient Chinese legend, the fenghuang appears only when reason, peace, and prosperity are prevailing in the country. A fenghuang's appearance was a sign that a new emperor would bring harmony to the country.

A modern sculpture shows the Chinese qilin looking more like a dragon than the horselike unicorn of most Western mythology.

The tortoise is another creature of Chinese mythology believed to have special symbolism. Because it is one of the oldest creatures on Earth, it is a symbol of longevity, strength, endurance, and wealth.

The unicorn, or *qilin*, is also a creature of good luck and longevity. The male qilin has a horn, but the female does not. The Chinese version of the unicorn looks much like a four-legged, hooved dragon. Legend says the last time a qilin showed itself was when Confucius was born. It has not appeared since.

GUN AND YU AND THE FLOODS

Many ancient civilizations told stories of a great flood, and ancient China is no exception. The Chinese had many problems with flooding in the areas near the Huang and Yangtze Rivers. The Chinese have more than one flood story, but the most common features Gun and his son, Yu.

According to Chinese mythology, many years ago, flooding swept through the countryside, covering even the mountains of China. Emperor Yao, a mythical emperor who was said to live in the 2400s BCE, was dismayed by all of the flooding. He asked the four mountains what he should do. The mountains told Yao his cousin Gun could help with the flooding.

Gun began trying to control the floodwaters. He stole *Xirang*, a self-expanding soil, from a god. He tried to use it to absorb the water. Gun built dams and embankments to control the flooding, but nothing seemed to stop the raging waters that destroyed the lands.

The Gods

The Chinese believed numerous gods inhabited the underworld, Earth, and heaven. In heaven, the Jade Emperor reigned supreme, but among the common people gods existed as well. The God of Walls and Moats protected each village. Each family received a god for protection, called the God of the Hearth. Another god, Guan Yu, protected fishermen. People worked to remain on the good side of the gods, worshiping them and offering them gifts. A life well lived might be rewarded with attainment of a godlike status in the afterlife.

After nine years of fighting the floods, Emperor Yao resigned. The new emperor, Shun, banished Gun because he had not been able to stop the flooding. Instead, Shun asked Gun's son, Yu, to help.

Yu asked a dragon and a tortoise for help. The creatures showed Yu what to do. Yu grabbed the rivers and rerouted them to the sea. He used the dragon's tail to cut ditches to guide the water away from the land. He dug canals, tunnels, and lakes to stop the flooding. Yu worked so hard he wore the nails off of his fingers and could no longer walk. However, because of his efforts, Yu became a demigod, or part god and part human.

ANCESTOR WORSHIP

The Chinese believed a person had two souls. One soul appeared at conception and died with the physical body. The higher soul, or spirit, formed at birth. When the body died, this spirit went to a heavenly place where it could watch over its descendants.

To protect its living descendants, the spirit required sacrifices offered in an ancestral temple. The living burned incense and offered food. If the spirit's physical body was not given enough offerings at the burial site, it would come back to haunt the living. Saying bad things about one's ancestors was the worst type of abusive language. It was believed the ancestors would come back and work evil on the living if they were not respected. Ancestral worship was most common in aristocratic Chinese society. This was because peasants did not have surnames, and therefore they did not have as strong a connection to ancestors to worship.

CONFUCIUS

Kongfuzi, better known by his Latinized name, Confucius, was one of the most important figures in ancient Chinese spirituality and philosophy. Confucius lived from 551 to 479 BCE, during the Zhou dynasty.

Confucius originated from Lu, in modern-day Shandong Province, where he worked in a government post. He sought out teachers to instruct him and eventually became a teacher himself. Confucius wanted to reform the Zhou culture and promote his moral teachings and a commitment to improving oneself. Confucius continued to gain higher offices, first becoming a magistrate and then a minister of justice. He left Lu looking for an emperor who would adopt his teachings, but he was never able to have a ruler fully adopt his principles while he was alive.

Confucius's philosophies, which became known as Confucianism, promoted principles of giving, trust, righteousness, appropriate behavior, and knowledge. He believed in always improving oneself and argued education should be easily available. Harmony among the people was more important than the rights of the individual. Confucius also explained, "never do unto another what you do not desire."[1] He edited the traditional Nine Classics.

After Confucius's death, his popularity grew. The Han dynasty made his tomb a temple, and a Song dynasty scholar compiled all of his teachings. Confucianism continued to be the main philosophical guide in Chinese government until the early 1900s.

TAOISM

Taoism, like Confucianism, began as a philosophy, not a religion. It influenced Chinese society through art and literature. Taoism was based on the teachings of Laozi, a philosopher who probably lived during the 500s BCE. Unlike Confucianism, Taoism emphasized the individual, rather than the group. Followers lived according to "The Way," or the force of Tao. The goal for those who practiced Taoism was finding a rhythm in the natural world. This rhythm could be achieved through a healthy diet and healthy habits such as meditation and martial arts, including Tai Chi.

Fêng Shui

Fêng shui literally means "wind and water."[2] The formal practice of fêng shui dates back to Zhou dynasty times, but it may have started earlier. Fêng shui studies the conditions of the spiritual and physical from the points of view of the spirits of earth, water, and wind. It is believed every place has its own *qi*, or spiritual breath, which can have a powerful effect on balance and harmony. The ancient Chinese believed graves, temples, and buildings should be built in connection with the principles of fêng shui. For example, houses and graves need to face the south because summer comes from that direction. Winter comes from the north and is not preferable. It is also preferred that pathways are not straight. This is said to slow down the qi, so it will not travel with full force.

BUDDHISM

Buddhism played another important role in ancient China. This way of life came to China from India during the Han dynasty. During the Tang dynasty, Buddhism spread all over the country. It is the most practiced religion in China today.

Buddhism is based on the teachings of the Buddha, a man named Siddhartha Gautama who probably lived in India in the 500s and 400s BCE. According to Buddhist teachings, Gautama eventually achieved enlightenment, or freedom from the pain and suffering of the physical world, and became the Buddha. Buddha stressed the desire to achieve wisdom and compassion. The ultimate goal of Buddhism is nirvana, or a state of total peace and release from all human suffering. One can achieve nirvana through meditation, prayer, performing good deeds, and disciplined behavior.

Buddhism saw mountains as sacred places, so temples and Buddhist monasteries were built there. Cave temples with Buddhist sculptures were built throughout northern China's mountains from roughly 300 to 400 CE. Empress Wu Zhao also promoted the building of many of the temples and cave sculptures.

The Longmen Caves in northeastern China are a series of Buddhist temples constructed between the 300s and 600s CE.

CHAPTER 7

TECHNOLOGICAL ADVANCES

B y the 1000s CE, ancient China was the most technically advanced civilization in the world. In fact, many of history's most important inventions have roots in China. The ancient Chinese were at the forefront of many advances in science, medicine, and technology. They developed the concept of mass production to manufacture more goods more quickly.

Advanced metallurgy made possible the bronze replica of Qin Shihuangdi's chariot excavated from his tomb.

Qin Shihuangdi used mass production techniques to create the thousands of terra-cotta warriors found in his tomb.

TRADITIONAL CHINESE MEDICINE

The ancient Chinese had a rich medical tradition. Traditional Chinese medicine relied on a combination of acupuncture, massage, herbs, diet, and heat therapy. Practitioners believed the body was made of the five elements: fire, water, metal, wood, and earth. These five elements must be balanced

Acupuncture

Acupuncture is one of the key practices of traditional Chinese medicine. It involves putting thin needles into the skin at various points on the body. The ancient Chinese believed, as do traditional Chinese medicine practitioners today, there are 365 points that are openings to the channels of the body where the qi flows. Acupuncturists insert needles into the openings to bring about healing. Acupuncture is most often used to treat pain and nausea.

Historians can trace the practice of acupuncture back to 1600 BCE. During the Song dynasty, bronze models of the human body were created with holes. The holes were filled with wax, and the model was filled with water. When in training, acupuncturists inserted the needles into the holes and water flowed out, indicating the proper placement of the needles.

The Chinese were not the only ones thought to have practiced acupuncture. Evidence of similar techniques has also been found in ancient Egypt, South Africa, and Yupik and Inuit cultures.

for full health. Patients were treated holistically and individually, based on their condition.

Mythical emperor Shen Nong Shi was credited with creating traditional Chinese medicine. According to Chinese legend, approximately 5,000 years ago Shen Nong Shi sampled hundreds of herbs in an attempt to figure out how they could be used as medicine. This information was passed down for many years and eventually written down after the Han dynasty. By 100 CE, doctors were using general anesthetic, made from plants and wine, to put patients to sleep during surgery. General anesthetic would not become widely used in the Western world for another 1,700 years.

COMPASS AND GUNPOWDER

Ancient China is known for many important inventions. Some of these, including the umbrella and the wheelbarrow, are still used around the world today. The compass was another such invention, dating to the 300s BCE. The first compasses were fish-shaped pieces of iron or large dipper-like spoons set on top of a bronze plate. They were not used for literal navigation, but rather for determining the best place to build in harmony with nature. Using lodestone, a natural magnet, the compass needle aligned itself with the magnetic field of the earth. By approximately 1050 CE, Chinese explorers were using compasses for navigation.

Gunpowder was another key Chinese invention. The Chinese discovered gunpowder in the 800s CE while trying to create a potion for immortality. The Tang dynasty used gunpowder in fireworks. During the Song dynasty, gunpowder propelled rockets used in military action. Eventually, gunpowder was used in guns and cannons.

PAPER

One of the greatest inventions of ancient China was paper. Cai Lun, a court eunuch during the Han dynasty, is credited with inventing paper, which he presented to Emperor Ho Ti in 105 CE.

Before the invention of paper, bamboo was used for writings. However, bamboo books were difficult to transport because they were so bulky. People sometimes wrote on silk, but it was expensive. Cai Lun

The ancient Chinese invented an early version of the compass thousands of years ago.

used tree bark, hemp, rags, and even fishnets to produce a lightweight, paperlike substance.

When it was first invented, paper was highly prized, and it was used only to record religious or other important writings, such as the sayings of Confucius. As it became more widely available, it was used for clothing and wrapping lacquer ware. The imperial family also used it for toilet paper. By the 200s CE, paper had become common in China. Traders sold paper along the Silk Road, making it a valuable export for China. In the 800s, Chinese warriors wore thick paper as armor because arrows could not go through it. Later, printed sheets were glued to walls and used as wallpaper.

PRINTING

The ancient Chinese invented not only paper but also the technology to print on it. This gave them the ability to produce multiple copies of works relatively easily. During the Warring States period, the Chinese used seals to stamp impressions on paper. They also made ink rubbings from inscriptions on carved stone. By the 600s CE, the Chinese used wood block printing on paper and silk. The printers first wrote the words on paper. They placed the paper on the wooden blocks and carved the characters into the wood. Ink could then be placed on the wood to easily print an impression on paper and silk.

A CLOSER LOOK

BAMBOO BOOKS

Before paper books, the Chinese used bamboo slips to keep records. They wrote on the bamboo slips vertically. In 2013, 15,000 bamboo slips were found in 11 wells in Hunan Province.[1] The bamboo slips reveal information about the records of wars from various dynasties, important government documents, and historical events. They also give information about the historical geographic names of various places. In addition to the important information written on them, the bamboo slips also provide details about the construction of the bamboo slips themselves and the art of calligraphy.

Today, ancient Chinese bamboo slips can be seen in museums. The extremely delicate artifacts are handled with care by museum staff. They are often placed under glass or even inside individual containers for extra protection.

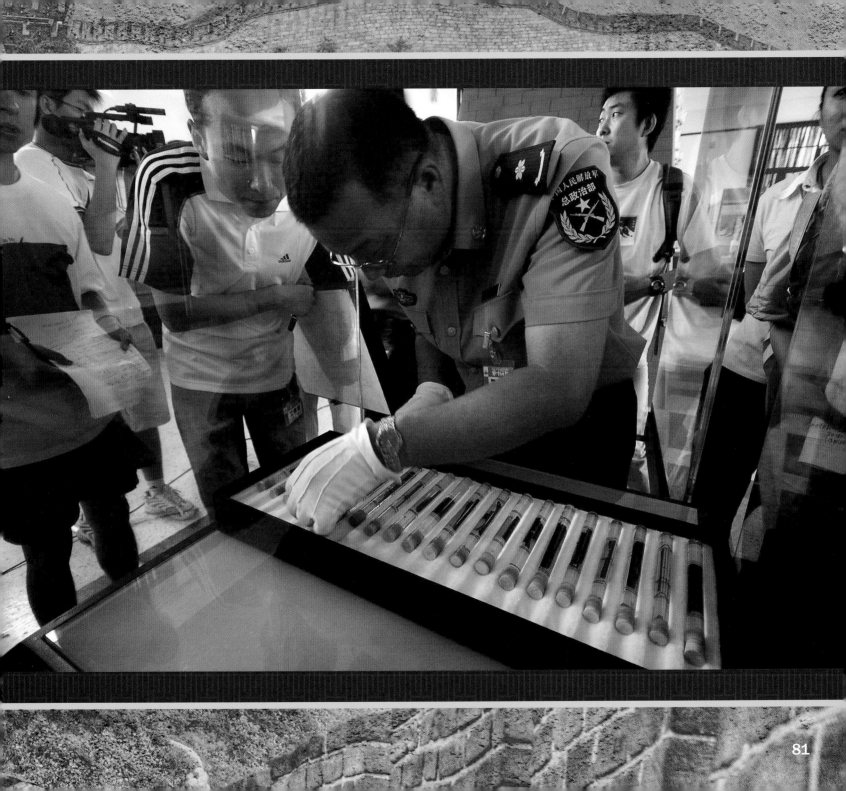

The wood blocks were made of fruitwoods, such as honey locust, boxwood, jujube, and pear trees. Printing blocks were passed down in families for centuries.

The first book was printed on a Buddhist scroll between 704 and 751 CE. More than 1 million copies were printed—a lot, even by modern standards.[2]

In the 1040s CE, Pi Sheng invented moveable type printing, using one character per block. Then these blocks, often made from bronze or wood, could be moved around and reused. Typesetters were often linguists, or masters of language, because there were so many Chinese characters they

Zhang Heng's Seismograph

Zhang Heng lived from 78 to 139 CE and is credited with many inventions tied to ancient China. One of his best-known inventions is the seismograph, a device that detects and measures earthquake vibrations. Earthquakes occur frequently in China, causing disruptions to food production. In ancient times, this sometimes triggered riots over food or rebellions against the government. It was important for ancient Chinese leaders to know when an earthquake had occurred, even if it was far enough away they could not feel it very strongly themselves.

Zhang Heng's device, invented in approximately 100 CE, was a bronze vase with eight bronze dragons holding balls in their mouths. Underneath the dragons were eight bronze toads with open mouths. If an earthquake occurred, the vibrations would cause the dragon facing in that direction to drop the ball into the mouth of one of the toads at the base of the vessel.

had to know. However, the Chinese rarely used moveable type printing because it was more expensive than woodblock printing due to the materials needed to make so many Chinese characters.

SCIENCE AND MATH

Scientists and mathematicians made great advances in their fields in ancient China, particularly in astronomy. Between 1000 and 600 BCE, astronomers used a circular device held up to the night sky, called a circumpolar constellation template. Astronomers oriented the template with the North Star in the center. The jagged edges around the device helped identify the constellations in the sky. The positions of the constellations could be used to determine the time. In 132 CE, court astronomer Zhang Heng invented

Zhang Heng's seismograph could detect vibrations in the earth stemming from earthquakes.

precursors to the modern clock. His device used hydropower to run an orrery, a mechanical model of the solar system. The astronomical clock could also be powered by liquid mercury instead of water, and it showed the position of the sun and parts of the solar system.

In the 1300s BCE, Chinese mathematicians were using a decimal system. By the 300s BCE, they had developed the concept of zero. By the 100s BCE, the Chinese recognized the use of negative numbers, which put them 1,700 years ahead of the Western world. In the 400s CE, mathematician Zu Chongzhi discovered how to calculate the solar year, predict eclipses,

Chopsticks

Chopsticks have been used in China since 1200 BCE. The first known chopsticks, made of bronze, were found in a tomb in Yin, near Anyang, in northeast China. The first chopsticks were very long and used for cooking. By approximately 300 BCE, following the Warring States period, people began using them for everyday eating. At this time, people trying to save on fueling costs often cut their uncooked food into small pieces so it would cook quickly. The chopsticks were the perfect utensils for picking up the small pieces.

Later chopsticks were made from bronze, ivory, jade, coral, and other materials and used by the wealthy. The most privileged could use expensive silver chopsticks. If the food were poisonous, they believed the silver would turn black. Chopsticks are still the primary utensils for eating in modern China.

and determine the value of pi, or the ratio of a circle's circumference to its diameter.

AGRICULTURAL TECHNOLOGY

Ancient Chinese science and technological advancements also improved Chinese agriculture practices. The ancient Chinese used ox-drawn wooden plows as early as the Neolithic times. By the 300s BCE, Chinese farmers grew crops in rows because one of the books describing farming suggested planting crops in rows would help them grow quicker and not interfere with one another.

Cast iron was not available in Europe until the 1300s CE, but in China it was used as early as the 300s BCE. Cast iron technology allowed the Chinese to create tools using iron ore. They melted and molded iron to make plows, hoes, knives, axes, and saws. Cast iron was not only for farming equipment; the Chinese also made statues, toys, and cooking utensils from cast iron.

The Wheelbarrow

The three-wheeled tool used in modern gardening may not seem like a huge technological advancement. But the wheelbarrow played an important role in ancient China. A man named Ko Yu is credited with inventing this practical tool as early as the first century BCE. The wheelbarrow allowed for easy transport of heavy supplies and even people. During warfare it was used to move food, equipment, and ammunition.

CHAPTER 8

WEAPONS AND DEFENSES

Confucius wanted to eliminate war altogether; however, even the rise of Confucianism did not eliminate conflict in ancient China. Chinese history is filled with battles and wars, often giving rise to new dynasties. During the Shang dynasty, wars were fought using guerrilla warfare—surprise attacks on the

The terra-cotta warriors and other artifacts found in Qin Shihuangdi's tomb have given historians a wealth of information about ancient Chinese weapons and warfare.

enemy. Historians believe many Shang conflicts involved land, particularly disputes over where animals would graze.

WAR OF UNIFICATION

Territorial rights and power struggles often led to wars between different groups. After thousands of years of skirmishes between dynasties and their armies, Qin Shihuangdi managed to successfully wage a war to make his army supreme. Qin Shihuangdi's tactics helped him conquer all of the states during his War of Unification.

Historians get a glimpse of what it might have been like to be in Qin Shihuangdi's army through letters written by his warriors. The letters detail how the more heads warriors cut off, the more promotions they received. If a soldier succeeded in winning a battle, he might be rewarded by being allowed to drink wine. If soldiers refused to obey an order, they were severely punished by a commanding officer.

MILITARY TECHNOLOGY

The ancient Chinese put their scientific knowledge to good use when crafting new weapons and military technology. In addition to developing gunpowder, Chinese inventors created several other useful weapons. The Chinese invented the crossbow during the 300s BCE. It was used as a weapon and to hunt animals. Archaeologists have learned about how many weapons were used, including the crossbow, by studying the statues and artifacts in Qin Shihuangdi's tombs. His tomb featured lines of terra-cotta soldiers holding crossbows. Some were kneeling and others were standing, suggesting the techniques real soldiers may have used. The standing soldiers could fire while protecting the soldiers who were kneeling and reloading their crossbows. Qin Shihuangdi's tomb also contained crossbow triggers rigged to let the arrows loose, an advanced technology for the time.

As bronze technology became available, the Chinese sword makers could create swords with sharp edges. An early version of the reel was also used in warfare. In 320 BCE, Chinese warriors threw javelins attached to cords. Because they wanted to reuse them, they reeled them back in for later use.

Arrowheads

When archaeologists excavated Qin Shihuangdi's tomb, they discovered thousands of arrowheads. The archaeologists also found that all of the arrowheads were very similar to one another, suggesting they had been mass-produced. Historians think this was done in a type of manufacturing assembly line.

89

In the 300s BCE, Chinese inventors developed a poisonous gas made by burning dried mustard and vegetable matter. Some cities contained underground tunnels used for hiding weapons and surprise attacks. Chinese armies pumped poisonous gases into tunnels in their enemies' cities. Soldiers coated arrows with poisons. Poison gases were also used for more practical purposes, such as getting rid of bookworms and other pests through home fumigation.

WALLS OF CHINA

One of ancient China's greatest efforts in military defense is also one of the most well-known symbols of China. The Great Wall's construction spanned

Booby Traps

The ancient Chinese used booby traps at least as early as Qin Shihuangdi's reign. In fact, archaeologists have not explored the inner tomb, where the emperor's body lies, because they know it is booby trapped. The craftsmen who helped with the construction were buried in the tomb with Qin Shihuangdi to guarantee they would not reveal the tomb's secrets. Even though archaeologists haven't opened Qin Shihuangdi's inner tomb because of safety concerns, they believe it is rigged with crossbows that will automatically shoot when the tomb is entered. The ceiling is supposedly decorated with jewels, and there are reportedly rivers and lakes made of mercury. Exposure to mercury could also potentially harm excavators. This ancient emperor, along with his workers, knew enough about warfare and surprise attack to continue puzzling modern investigators.

While the Great Wall was started in ancient times, most of it was constructed more recently.

more than 1,000 years and many dynasties. However, the ancient Chinese had built walls for more than 1,000 years before the famous one was even started. Many dynasties built walls to protect themselves from groups of nomads. Historians now claim most of the walls built in defense were militarily ineffective. The walls were not linked together, so enemies simply climbed the walls or went around them.

Built in stages, the Great Wall began during the Qin dynasty. During that time, workers built the wall from soil pounded into shape using a frame. This simple technique of construction can still be seen in China's rural areas today. The Great Wall seen today was completed by the Ming dynasty (1368–1644 CE). Today the Great Wall of China twists and turns for approximately 5,500 miles (8,800 km).[2]

CHAPTER 9

CHINA'S LEGACY

China's inventions have contributed to many modern advances still used today. China spread its ideas about culture and technology to other lands through trading. Arabic peoples often traded with the Chinese and then took Chinese wares to Europe.

Many Chinese festivals, such as the Chinese New Year, are still celebrated around the world.

The Tang Barbie

Archaeologists find many treasures from ancient times that give them glimpses into the culture and the people of China. Even artifacts from graves and bone inscriptions used in divinations reveal much information about people. One archaeological dig unearthed a statue of a woman, beautifully dressed, whose arms were made of paper tickets from a pawn shop during the Tang dynasty. The tickets include addresses of people and the amounts of money they borrowed. She was found in a gravesite at Turfan, in northwest China. The curators at the Metropolitan Museum of Art called her the "Tang Barbie" because she was the same size as an American Barbie doll and wore elaborate fashions.[1] No one knows exactly why figurines like these ended up in the grave.

From major technological advancements, such as gunpowder, paper, printing, and the compass, to other inventions such as wheelbarrows and chopsticks, ancient China made a huge impact on the larger world. The Tang and Song dynasties were the most technologically advanced in the world at their time, and many of their inventions were not used in the rest of the world for hundreds of years after their inventions in China. But as trade and travelers spread information about Chinese inventions, the rest of the world built on and improved Chinese inventions.

After the Mongols took over China after the Song dynasty, six dynasties ruled China. During the Ming dynasty, from 1368 to 1644 CE, China began cutting itself off from the rest of the world. Europe became a powerful region, colonizing other areas around the world.

Dynastic rule continued in China until 1911, when the imperial government ended and modern China began. In 1949, China became known as the People's Republic of China and came under Communist rule.

ANCIENT CHINA'S LEGACY

The ancient Chinese are remembered for their contributions to art, philosophy, literature, and science. The Qin dynasty's efforts to centralize the government and military continue to impress modern historians. The Han dynasty brought forth great accomplishments, including porcelain and paper. The Chinese philosophies of Confucianism, Buddhism, and Taoism focused on the best ways to live a prosperous life. These beliefs are still prevalent throughout China and the world today.

Modern culture is still affected by ancient China. The English custom of tea drinking, which spread to North America, originated in China. Chopsticks, rice, and the Chinese zodiac can easily be found in Western cultures. Modern pastimes such as playing cards and celebrating with fireworks came from China. Porcelain is still a prized possession for modern families. Chinese immigrants to Western

Inoculations

An inoculation is a shot that contains a live virus. The hope is the patient will develop immunity to it. Europeans began developing vaccinations for smallpox in 1796 CE. However, historical records show the Chinese had been inoculating against the deadly disease hundreds of years earlier. Chinese physicians experimented with taking the virus from those who had become immune to the disease.

Chinese Food

In Western cultures, Chinese food has permeated many small towns and big cities in Chinese restaurants. Restaurants bring many of the foods and cooking techniques of China to Western society. One such technique, stir-fry, in which meat and vegetables are cut very small to cook fast, has its roots in ancient China and is still very popular today. Soybeans, millet, and tea are just some of the foods from ancient China that are incorporated in Western diets.

countries and their descendants celebrate Chinese holidays, such as Chinese New Year.

Today China is one of the most powerful countries in the world and a leader in industry, business, and technology. But the Chinese have not forgotten the foundation modern China is built on. Remnants of the ancient Chinese civilization can be seen throughout modern China. Tourists can still be amazed by Qin Shihuangdi's terra-cotta soldiers, walk the Great Wall of China, and visit dozens of ancient Chinese cities steeped in history. China's ancient technologies continue to influence our world today.

Archaeologists continue making discoveries about ancient China as they excavate tombs and other historic sites.

TIMELINE

10,000 BCE
Humans first settle in the region that is now China.

2100 BCE–1600 BCE
Historical but inconclusive documents suggest the Xia dynasty ruled ancient China.

C. 1600 BCE
The Shang dynasty comes into power and rules ancient China until 1046 BCE.

1046 BCE
The Zhou dynasty overthrows the Shang dynasty, ruling until 256 BCE.

770 BCE–476 BCE
Many small states struggle for power in ancient China during an era known as the Spring and Autumn period.

551 BCE
Confucius is born; his way of thinking will spur the popular way of life known as Confucianism.

475 BCE–221 BCE
China's various states battle one another in what becomes known as the Warring States period.

C. 300s BCE
The compass is invented.

221 BCE

Qin Shihuangdi unites ancient
China under the Qin dynasty.

690

Empress Wu Zhao becomes
China's only female emperor.

206 BCE

The Han dynasty comes into power.

C. 800s

The ancient Chinese invent gunpowder.

C. 100 CE

Zhang Heng invents the seismograph.

960

The Song dynasty begins ruling China.

618–907

Art and literature flourish
under the Tang dynasty.

1974

Farmers digging a well discover
Qin Shihuangdi's tomb full of
thousands of terra-cotta warriors.

ANCIENT HISTORY

KEY DATES

- 475–221 BCE: During the Warring States period, seven factions vie for power in ancient China.

- 221 BCE: Qin Shihuangdi completes his conquest of ancient China.

- 618–907 CE: Cultural developments, including poetry, pottery, and the invention of the printed book, mark the reign of the Tang dynasty.

KEY TOOLS AND TECHNOLOGIES

- Ancient Chinese inventors developed the compass, the seismograph, gunpowder, paper, and printing well before Western civilizations.

- The ancient Chinese made many advancements in the areas of military technologies, mathematics, and medicine, including the crossbow and inoculation against deadly diseases.

LANGUAGES

The Chinese written language has been in use for more than 3,500 years. Ancient Chinese writing used a complex system of pictographs featuring thousands of characters.

KEY DYNASTIES

Xia dynasty* (2100–1600 BCE)

Shang dynasty (1600–1046 BCE)

Zhou dynasty (1046–256 BCE)

Qin dynasty (221–206 BCE)

Han dynasty (206 BCE–220 CE)

Tang dynasty (618–907 CE)

Song dynasty (960–1279 CE)

*Archaeologists have not proven the existence of the Xia dynasty.

IMPACT OF THE CHINESE CIVILIZATION

- The Silk Road, built by the Chinese, allowed ancient China to share its ideas with many Western societies, including Rome.

- Ancient China developed the civil service examination for those seeking government posts. Many modern governments still require such an examination today.

- Many of ancient China's scientific achievements, such as the seismograph and compass, were later adopted by the Western world. Modern versions of these early inventions are still used today.

- Qin Shihuangdi created a unified currency, standardized weights, measures, and writing. Most governments today also use unified systems.

QUOTE

"The Chinese had a very cultured and civilized society. Song Dynasty silks, for example, were remarkably advanced. The Chinese were using very sophisticated looms with up to 1,800 moving parts. China was simply far more developed technologically and culturally than any state in the West."

— *Robin Yates, China expert*

GLOSSARY

acupuncture
A traditional Chinese practice of inserting needles at certain points on the body to alleviate pain or other ailments.

calligraphy
A type of script writing considered an art form in ancient China.

canal
A manmade waterway used for transportation.

Communist
A form of government in which the government owns the means of production.

concubine
A mistress.

Confucianism
A philosophy in ancient China based on the teachings of Confucius.

dynasty
A family that controls a country for a long period of time through successive rulers.

fêng shui
In ancient China, a way of studying the spiritual and physical conditions before building a structure or choosing a burial site.

jade
A green stone often used to make jewelry and other goods.

mass production
The process of making something in large quantities.

millet
An ancient grass grown in northern China; its seeds were a food staple.

Neolithic
The era of ancient history when stone tools were common.

nomad
A person who travels from place to place to find food and resources, rather than living permanently in one area.

oracle
A person believed able to communicate with the gods and ancestors and relay their advice or messages.

pagoda
A type of tower with many stories and a spire on the top.

Taoism
An ancient Chinese philosophy based on the teachings of Laozi.

ADDITIONAL RESOURCES

SELECTED BIBLIOGRAPHY

Fenby, Jonathan. *China's Imperial Dynasties: 1600 BC–AD 1912*. New York: Metro, 2008. Print.

Scarpari, Maurizio. *Ancient China: Chinese Civilization from the Origins to the Tang Dynasty*. New York: Barnes & Noble, 2006. Print.

Yuan, Haiwang. *This Is China: The First 5,000 Years*. Great Barrington, MA: Berkshire, 2010. Print.

FURTHER READINGS

Bailey, Diane. *Emperor Qin's Terra-Cotta Army*. Minneapolis: Abdo, 2015. Print.

Challen, Paul C. *Hail! Ancient Chinese*. New York: Crabtree, 2011. Print.

Liu-Perkins, Christine, and Sarah S. Brannen. *At Home in Her Tomb: Lady Dai and the Ancient Chinese Treasures of Mawangdui*. Watertown, MA: Charlesbridge, 2014. Print.

Morley, Jacqueline, and David Antram. *You Wouldn't Want to Work on the Great Wall of China!: Defenses You'd Rather Not Build*. New York: Franklin Watts, 2006. Print.

WEBSITES

To learn more about Ancient Civilizations, visit **booklinks.abdopublishing.com**. These links are routinely monitored and updated to provide the most current information available.

PLACES TO VISIT

ASIAN ART MUSEUM

200 Larkin Street

San Francisco, CA 94012

415-581-3500

http://www.asianart.org

This museum holds one of the largest collections of Asian art in the world, with artifacts dating back more than 6,000 years.

FREER-SACKLER GALLERIES OF ART, SMITHSONIAN INSTITUTION

1050 Independence Avenue Southwest

Washington, DC 20013

202-633-1000

http://www.asia.si.edu

The Freer and Sackler museums specialize in Asian art. They have more than 10,000 Chinese artifacts dating from Neolithic times to the present day.

SOURCE NOTES

Chapter 1. China's First Emperor

1. Yuan Haiwang. *This Is China: The First 5,000 Years*. Great Barrington, MA: Berkshire, 2010. Print. 29.

2. *China's First Emperor*. Dir. Andreas Gutzeit. Perf. David Shih, Narrator. A&E Home Video, History Channel, 2008. DVD.

3. "Han Ethnic Group." *ChinaCulture.org*. ChinaCulture.org, n.d. Web. 5 Sept. 2014.

4. "China's Age of Invention." *NOVA*. WGBH Educational Foundation, 2014. Web. 5 Sept. 2014.

Chapter 2. A Long History

1. Yuan Haiwang. *This Is China: The First 5,000 Years*. Great Barrington, MA: Berkshire, 2010. Print. 20–21.

2. "Public Summary Request of the People's Republic of China to the Government of the United States Under Article 9 of the 1970 UNESCO Convention." *Bureau of Education and Cultural Affairs Exchange Programs*. US Department of State, 17 Dec. 2004. Web. 17 June 2014.

Chapter 3. Imperial Government

1. "Silk Road." *Encyclopaedia Britannica*. Encyclopaedia Britannica, 2014. Web. 5 Sept. 2014.

2. Patricia Buckley Ebrey. *The Cambridge Illustrated History of China*. New York: Cambridge UP, 1996. Print. 54.

3. "Paper Money." *Silk Road*. Silk Road Foundation, n.d. Web. 2 Aug. 2014.

4. Patricia Buckley Ebrey. *The Cambridge Illustrated History of China*. New York: Cambridge UP, 1996. Print. 116–117.

Chapter 4. Life in Ancient China

1. "Chang'an." *Encyclopedia of China.* Facts on File, 1998. Web. 24 Sept. 2014.

2. Robert K. G. Temple. *The Genius of China: 3,000 Years of Science, Discovery, and Invention.* New York: Simon, 2007. Print. 130.

Chapter 5. Artistic Treasures

1. Patricia Buckley Ebrey. *The Cambridge Illustrated History of China.* New York: Cambridge UP, 1996. Print. 26.

2. Behzad Bavarian. "Unearthing Technology's Influence on the Ancient Chinese Dynasties through Metallurgical Investigations." *Unearthing Technology's Influence on the Ancient Chinese Dynasties through Metallurgical Investigations* (2005): n. pag. California State University Northridge, July 2005. Web. 2 Aug. 2014.

3. Alison Bailey, Ronald G. Knapp, et al. *China.* London: DK, 2007. Print. 89.

SOURCE NOTES CONTINUED

Chapter 6. Religion, Philosophy, and Mythology

1. Yi Shen. "Chinese History and Culture—1400 BC–89 AD: Ancient China." N.p., 2011. Web. 25 May 2014.

2. Paul Carus. *Chinese Astrology*. LaSalle, IL: Open Court, 1974. Print. 55.

Chapter 7. Technological Advances

1. Kaihao Wang. "History Unearthed." *China Culture*. Ministry of Culture, P.R.C., 17 Apr. 2014. Web. 18 June 2014.

2. Robert K. G. Temple. *The Genius of China: 3,000 Years of Science, Discovery, and Invention*. New York: Simon, 1986. Print. 112.

Chapter 8. Weapons and Defenses

1. Sun Tzu. *The Art of* War. Trans. Lionel Giles. *Classics MIT*. Daniel C. Stevenson, Web Atomics, 2009. Web. 5 Sept. 2014.

2. "Great Wall of China." *Encyclopaedia Britannica*. Encyclopaedia Britannica, 2014. Web. 5 Sept. 2014.

Chapter 9. China's Legacy

1. James B. Wiener. "Trading Cultures along the Silk Road: An Interview with Professor Valerie Hansen." *Ancient History Encyclopedia*. Jan Van Der Crabben, 3 Mar. 2013. Web. 15 June 2014.